The Power Cut

Mick Manning
and Brita Granström

W
FRANKLIN WATTS

For Chloë, Lesley and Spencer with love

First published in 2002
by Franklin Watts,
96 Leonard Street,
London EC2A 4XD

Franklin Watts Australia
56 O'Riordan Street
Alexandria
NSW 2015

The illustrations in this book have
been drawn by Brita

Text and illustrations © 2002 Mick Manning
and Brita Granström
Series editor: Rachel Cooke
Art director: Jonathan Hair

Printed in Hong Kong, China
A CIP catalogue record is available from
the British Library.
Dewey Classification 621.31
ISBN 0 7496 4300 5

Contents

A windy day

It was cold,
wet and windy.
A day for staying
in - TV, toast,
hot drinks and
a warm fire . . .

*Electricity powers lots of
things. All we have to do
is 'plug in' to the mains.
WARNING: mains electricity
is dangerous. Never play
with sockets or wires.*

7

The wind
moaned, the
sky grew dark.
Mum switched
on the lights.

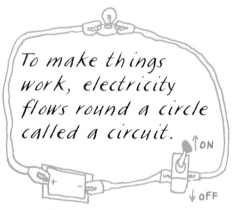

To make things
work, electricity
flows round a circle
called a circuit.

↑ON
↓OFF

Switch on, electricity flows
and the light works.

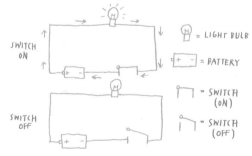

SWITCH
ON

SWITCH
OFF

= LIGHT BULB

+ − = BATTERY

= SWITCH
(ON)

= SWITCH
(OFF)

Switch off, the circuit is
broken and electricty stops
flowing. The light goes out.

8

9

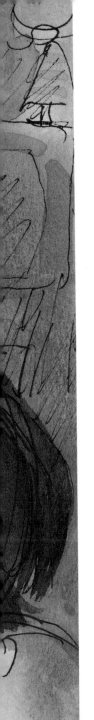

Lights out!

Suddenly - crash, bang, lights out! No TV - no sound! No kettle - no hot drinks! No fire - no warmth! No light!

Can you imagine a world without electricity?
The machines it powers give us sound, heat and light.
Electric fridges and freezers make things cold.

It was a power cut.
Someone rang Dad.
'A tree's come down
on the power
cables,' he said.

Mains electricity flows
along cables from
the power station
where it is
made.

Sometimes an
accident will
break a cable
and stop the
flow - just
like a
switch.

Candles

Dad had to go to work. We had a cold tea - by candle-light.

People have used electric power for less than **200** years. Before that, they used candles and oil lamps to see in the dark.

Torches

Mum found two torches. She checked the freezer. I checked our tropical fish. We thought about Dad in the rain . . .

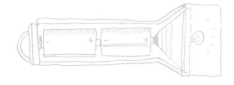

Torches run on batteries. Batteries store small amounts of electricity so you don't need to use the mains.

What other machines use batteries to work?

17

We wrapped ourselves in blankets and Mum told stories. Dad was busy, too.

Only specially-trained engineers can mend power cables. They must be very careful.

Look out for this sign. It warns you that dangerous electricity is nearby. Don't go close, don't play nearby and DON'T TOUCH!

The torches went out.
No more batteries!
The candles
flickered and died.
It was dark
and scary . . .
'How much longer?'
we wondered.

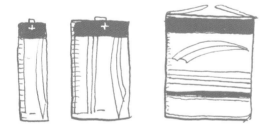

Batteries do not last forever.
The store of electricity
in them runs out.
We say they go flat.

Power's back!

Then, click!
Just like that, the
lights came back on.
And everything else
as well - TV, kettle,
freezer, fish tank . . .

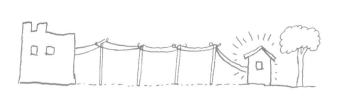

Once the power cables
are mended, the
electricity can flow
again from the power
station to our homes.

Dad came home
and we all had
hot drinks.

Power stations are
working day and night
so we can have
electricity whenever we
want it – unless there
is a power cut!

I went to bed
and switched
off the light.

It was nice to
know I could
turn it on again
- with just the
flick of a switch.

27

Electric ideas

Find out more about electricity.

A closer look

Take out the batteries from a torch. Note the way they fitted in. Try them the wrong way round. Does the torch still work? Is there only one way the batteries work?

Take a closer look at the torch bulb, too. Which bit of it do you think lights up?

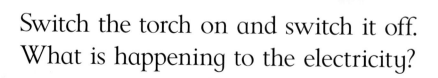

Switch the torch on and switch it off. What is happening to the electricity?

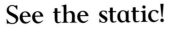

See the static!
Rub a balloon against a woolly jumper. Put the balloon against the wall or ceiling and it stays there.

Rub another balloon and hold it above your head. Your hair is pulled up to the balloon.

When you rub the balloon, you make a kind of electricity called static electricity. This pulls the balloon to the wall and your hair to the balloon.

Safety
The tiny amount of electricity in a torch battery or on a balloon is safe to play with. But never play with mains electricity or plug sockets, or go near where you see this sign.

Electricity words and index

battery A special tube or box that stores a supply of electricity. Pages 8, 16, 20

cable A thick rope of wires twisted together. Cables are used to carry mains electricity. Pages 12, 19, 22

circuit The circle electricity flows around. Page 8

engineers People who are specially trained to design, build and mend machines. Page 19

mains electricity Electricity made in power stations that flows along cables into our homes. Pages 7, 12, 16

power cut When the supply of mains electricity is stopped, usually because of an accident. Pages 12, 25

power station The place where mains electricity is made. Pages 12, 22, 25

plug A part that connects machines that use electricity to the mains electricity supply. Page 7

socket A place in the wall where machines can be attached with a plug to the mains electricity supply. Page 7

switch An electrical part which controls the flow of electricity around a circuit. You turn a switch on to make something work. Pages 8, 12, 26